THE PRINCE – FOR EVERYONE

NICCOLÒ MACHIAVELLI

Translated by
W. K. MARRIOTT
Edited by
RICHARD ENLOW

FOR EVERYONE BOOKS

Legal Notice & Copyright Information

This book is based on *The Prince* by Niccolò Machiavelli, a work in the public domain. However, the adaptation, modernization, and restructured presentation of this material are protected under copyright law.

All rights to this adapted work, including its unique phrasing, formatting, and editorial enhancements, are reserved by the copyright holder. No part of this book may be reproduced, distributed, or transmitted in any form or by any means—electronic, mechanical, or otherwise—without prior written permission from the publisher, except for brief quotations used in reviews or as permitted by applicable copyright law.

For permissions, inquiries, or additional information, please contact the publisher:

For Everyone Books

info@foreveryonebooks.com

A NOTE ON THE TEXT & THIS ADAPTATION

This book is a simplified version of *The Prince*. Originally written by Niccolò Machiavelli in 1513, *The Prince* explores the nature of power, leadership, and strategy. While its lessons remain relevant, the language and style of the original can feel dense and difficult for modern readers.

This adaptation stays true to Machiavelli's core ideas—on ruling, influence, and political survival—but presents them in a clearer, more accessible way. The goal is to make these insights easy to understand and apply, so that anyone can learn from Machiavelli's wisdom and use it to navigate leadership, decision-making, and power dynamics in today's world.

INTRODUCTION

What does it mean to be "Machiavellian"? Many think it means being ruthless or manipulative. The term now often stands for corruption and cold ambition. But this isn't a fair view of Machiavelli or *The Prince*.

When Niccolò Machiavelli wrote this book over 500 years ago, he wasn't promoting evil. He was explaining how power truly operates. He witnessed good rulers overthrown by those who played the game better. Machiavelli knew that leaders who only strive to be kind often fail. This isn't because kindness is wrong, but because the world doesn't always reward it.

Machiavelli believed the strongest leaders see reality as it is, not as they wish it to be. That's why his lessons remain relevant today.

Why *The Prince* Still Matters

You don't have to be a king or politician to learn from *The Prince*. Machiavelli's lessons on power, leadership, and influence are relevant in many areas. They impact business, relationships, social dynamics, and personal choices.

Look at modern politics. Leaders rise and fall not just because of their ideas, but also how well they manage perception. A politician who seems weak—regardless of their good policies—will lose support. A CEO who hesitates will see their company fail. A movement that lacks strategy will be overtaken by one that has it.

These ideas also apply in daily life. Machiavelli reminds us that people often act out of self-interest, fear, or opportunity. They do not consider fairness or gratitude. Understanding this doesn't mean being ruthless; it means being realistic. Understanding how power works can help you gain an advantage. This knowledge is useful for negotiating a raise, starting a business, or making better choices.

Making *The Prince* Easier to Understand

Despite its insights, *The Prince* isn't easy to read. The original text is dense, with archaic words and references that may confuse modern readers. This edition aims to make Machiavelli's ideas clear and direct. It keeps the original meaning while being easy to understand.

The text has been simplified so every reader can grasp what Machiavelli really meant. Each chapter includes modern reflections that link his lessons to today's world. These are more than summaries. They explain how to use his ideas in real-life situations like politics, business, personal choices, and leadership.

How to Read *The Prince*

You don't have to agree with everything Machiavelli says. Some people disagree with his ideas. They challenge our beliefs about leadership and morality. But that's why this book is valuable. It pushes us to think.

Read *The Prince* not as a rulebook, but as a guide to understanding power—how people gain it, lose it, and survive in an unfair world. Some of his ideas may seem harsh, yet they reflect real patterns in human behavior that still hold true.

As you read, ask yourself: Where do these lessons appear in today's world? How do they relate to your life? How can understanding power help you make smarter decisions?

That's what *The Prince* is truly about. And that's why, 500 years later, it remains one of the most important books ever written.

—Richard Enlow

Original Dedication

People often gift rulers items they value or think the ruler will like. These gifts include fine horses, weapons, gold, and other precious things. Wishing to show my devotion to Your Highness, I searched for my most valuable possession. I found that nothing is more precious to me than the knowledge I have gained from studying great leaders and history.

After much thought, I have condensed these lessons into a small book, which I now present to you. Though I know this book is unworthy of your greatness, I trust in your wisdom and generosity to accept it. In its pages, you will find lessons that took me years to understand, now offered to you in a form that can be grasped quickly.

I have not dressed up this work with elegant language or unnecessary embellishments, as some writers do. Instead, I have let the weight of its ideas and the importance of its subject speak for themselves. Some might say it is bold for someone of my humble status to offer advice on ruling. But just as a painter must step back to see the full picture, a ruler must look beyond the palace walls to truly understand their people. To guide wisely, one must see both the heights of power and the struggles of everyday life.

So, I ask you to accept this small gift in the spirit in which it is offered. If you read it carefully, you will see my greatest hope: that you achieve the greatness your fortune and virtues promise. From your high position, you may see how fortune has treated me unfairly. Yet, you will also recognize the valuable lessons I have gained through these hardships.

1

LEADERSHIP TRANSITIONS & STABILITY

In history, there are two key types of governments: republics and principalities. Principalities fall into two main types:

1. Hereditary Principalities – Power is held by a single ruling family over many generations.
2. New Principalities – A ruler gains control over a state not previously ruled by his family.

New principalities can be:

- Entirely new states – Built from scratch, like Milan under Francesco Sforza.
- Annexed territories – These are regions added to a domain, such as Naples joining the Spanish crown.

Newly acquired lands may:

- Be used to living under a prince, making them easier to rule.
- Have a history of freedom, making them harder to control.

How Rulers Gain Power

A prince can acquire a state through:

- Fortune – Inheritance, luck, or outside support.
- Ability – Military strength, political skill, or strategy.

∼

Modern Reflections on Chapter 1: Leadership Transitions & Stability

Leadership changes occur in politics, business, and organizations in much the same way. A leader taking over a strong system, like a family business or a long-term government, has fewer challenges. But a leader taking over an unstable or entirely new system must work much harder to gain legitimacy. This applies to CEOs, startup founders, and political leaders. Recognizing the nature of one's leadership role helps in crafting a strategy for long-term influence.

2

HEREDITARY PRINCIPALITIES

I won't talk about republics here since I've written about them elsewhere. Instead, I'll focus on principalities—how rulers keep control and stay in power.

Why Hereditary Principalities Are Easier to Keep

A state ruled by the same family for generations is easier to hold onto because:

- People are used to the ruling family and accept their leadership.
- If the prince follows tradition and makes smart changes, he can keep power.
- Even if he is kicked out, he has a good chance of getting power back if the new ruler struggles.

Example: The Duke of Ferrara

The Duke of Ferrara maintained control of his state despite facing challenges from the Venetians in 1484 and Pope Julius II in 1510. Because his family had ruled for generations, the people remained loyal to him.

The Benefits of Being a Hereditary Prince

A prince who inherits power:

- Doesn't have to make big, risky changes to prove himself.
- Is naturally more respected, as long as he doesn't make major mistakes.

New rulers, on the other hand, have to change things to gain control, which can upset people. But when a family has ruled for a long time, old problems are often forgotten, making it easier to stay in power.

Modern Reflections on Chapter 2: Hereditary Principalities

1. People Trust What They Know
Machiavelli says families that have ruled for generations find it easier to stay in power. People are familiar with them.

This is true in businesses and politics today. For instance, Coca-Cola and Apple enjoy strong trust in their brands. New businesses, however, must work hard to build that trust.

The lesson? Familiarity breeds acceptance. But even long-time leaders must be cautious. Too many mistakes can lead people to seek change.

2. Change Brings Risk—But Also Opportunity

When a new leader takes over, they don't need to make big changes to hold power. Sudden shifts can cause unease. A prince inheriting power should respect traditions and make only small improvements.

This still holds today. If a new CEO takes over a well-known company, rapid changes can upset customers and employees. By carefully improving what works, they can lead effectively.

3. A Strong Reputation Can Help You Bounce Back

Machiavelli notes that even if a hereditary prince is ousted, he can often regain power. Why? People are familiar with his family's leadership. We see this in modern politics when well-known leaders return after losing elections.

The takeaway? A solid reputation helps a leader endure tough times. However, that reputation must be built on trust. Losing it makes recovery difficult.

3

MIXED PRINCIPALITIES

The Challenges of Ruling a Newly Conquered Land

When a ruler takes over new territory and adds it to his existing state (a "mixed principality"), he faces major problems. At first, people may welcome him, especially if they were unhappy with the previous ruler. But once they face changes—such as new taxes, stricter laws, or a foreign military presence—their loyalty fades.

This leads to two issues:

1. The new ruler creates enemies among those hurt by the takeover.
2. He disappoints those who helped him, as he can't meet all their expectations.

Because of this instability, a new ruler must work harder to keep power than one who inherits a long-standing kingdom. Louis XII of France learned this the hard way when he took control of Milan but quickly lost it. The same people who supported him at first later turned against him.

Why a Second Rebellion Is Harder to Stop

If a ruler loses control of a new land and later takes it back, he must act more forcefully to secure it. A rebellion gives him an excuse to remove enemies and strengthen his rule.

Louis XII lost Milan twice. The first time, he faced only minor resistance. The second time, he had to fight a much stronger opposition, proving that if a ruler doesn't secure his power early, his problems will only grow.

How to Keep Control of a Conquered Land

Newly acquired territories will either:

- Share the ruler's language and customs, making them easier to govern.
- Have a different culture and laws, making them harder to control.

If the new land is culturally similar, the ruler should:

- Eliminate the former ruling family to prevent any claims to power.
- Keep the same laws and taxes so life feels familiar.

France used this approach in Burgundy, Brittany, and Normandy, which became stable parts of the kingdom.

If the new land is culturally different, the ruler should:

- Move there himself to quickly handle problems and show strong leadership. The Ottoman sultans did this in Greece to keep control.
- Establish colonies to secure key areas. Colonists are loyal to the ruler, and since only a few people are displaced, the majority remain peaceful.

Keeping a large army in a conquered land is a bad idea—it's expensive and makes people resentful. Soldiers disrupt daily life and create enemies, while colonies provide security with less resistance.

Controlling Neighboring Powers

A ruler must also think about surrounding states. He should:

- Support weaker neighbors to gain their loyalty.
- Keep stronger rivals in check.
- Prevent powerful outsiders from interfering, since local factions often invite them in.

The Romans used this strategy in Greece by supporting weaker groups like the Achaeans while weakening powerful enemies like Macedon. This balance prevented any single force from challenging their rule.

The Danger of Waiting Too Long

Machiavelli compares political problems to a disease: easy to cure when caught early, but deadly if ignored. A wise ruler acts swiftly—hesitation allows small issues to grow into crises.

The Romans acted early by attacking potential threats like Philip of Macedon before he could invade Italy. In contrast, many modern rulers make the mistake of hoping problems will solve themselves.

France's Mistakes in Italy

Louis XII of France made several key errors when ruling Italy:

- He weakened his allies instead of protecting them.
- He strengthened the Church, which gained more power.
- He invited Spain into Italy, creating a dangerous rival.
- He did not live in the region, making his rule weaker.
- He relied on an army instead of setting up colonies, which led to resentment.

His worst mistake was allowing the destruction of Venice, which had acted as a buffer between him and his enemies. Once Venice was gone, France was more vulnerable.

The Danger of Helping Others Gain Power

The key lesson:

"He who makes another powerful ruins himself."

Louis XII helped Spain and the Pope become stronger in Italy, but they later turned against him. By boosting their power, he weakened his own position, leading to his downfall.

Final Lesson

A ruler who takes over new territory must act quickly and decisively to secure control. He should:

- Remove rivals.
- Keep existing laws to avoid upsetting people.
- Either live in the region or set up colonies to maintain order.
- Balance power among neighboring states and prevent outsiders from interfering.
- Never let an ally become too strong, or they may turn into a future enemy.

France failed to follow these rules in Italy—and lost everything as a result.

Modern Reflections on Chapter 3: Mixed Principalities

1. People Welcome Change—Until It Affects Them

Machiavelli points out that a new leader may be welcomed at first, especially if the old ruler was disliked. But once new laws, taxes, or rules come into play, opinions often change.

This is evident in today's business and politics. People may cheer for a new CEO or president, but if changes like layoffs or new policies affect them, they may quickly turn against that leader. The lesson? Gaining support is easy at first, but keeping it takes careful leadership.

2. Second Chances Are Harder Than First Chances

If a new ruler loses power and tries to reclaim it, the opposition will be stronger. Those who were undecided will now unite against him. Machiavelli warns that a failed first attempt makes a second harder.

We see this in business when a new product flops. Convincing customers to try again is tough. In politics, a leader who loses credibility struggles to regain public trust. The key takeaway? The first chance at leadership is crucial—don't waste it.

3. Smart Leaders Secure Power Early

Machiavelli tells new leaders to act fast. They should remove threats, earn trust, and build a strong government. In today's business world, when one company buys another, leaders must act fast. They need to establish new management, clarify expectations, and eliminate any roadblocks.

A common mistake is delaying problem-solving. Machiavelli warns that small issues can escalate if ignored. The best leaders act swiftly before opposition can organize.

4

WHY ALEXANDER'S SUCCESSORS KEPT CONTROL OF PERSIA

Why Didn't Persia Rebel After Alexander's Death?

Alexander the Great quickly conquered the huge Persian Empire. Even after his death, his generals kept control. Normally, when a ruler dies or is removed, people try to take back their land. But this didn't happen in Persia. The only real struggles were between Alexander's own generals, who fought each other for more power.

Different Ways States Are Governed

To understand why Persia didn't rebel, we need to look at two ways rulers govern their lands:

1. A single ruler with appointed officials

- The ruler has total control, and his officials serve only because he allows them to.
- They can be replaced at any time and have no personal power.
- Example: The Ottoman Empire (modern-day Turkey). The Sultan had complete control. He appointed local governors and could remove them anytime.

2. A ruler with powerful nobles

- The ruler shares power with wealthy barons or lords.
- These nobles own land, have influence, and are respected by the people.
- Example: France, where kings had to work with strong noble families who held power for generations.

Which Type of State Is Harder to Conquer?

- A state with one powerful ruler (like the Ottoman Empire) is hard to invade but easy to rule.

  - Since all power is in the hands of one ruler, invaders can't find local allies to help them.
  - To win, you must completely defeat the ruler in battle.

○ But once he is gone, there are no powerful nobles to resist the new ruler, making it easier to govern.

- A decentralized state (like France) is easy to invade but hard to rule.

  ○ A foreign invader can find unhappy nobles to help overthrow the king.
  ○ But after winning, the new ruler faces trouble. The remaining nobles still have power and might rebel.
  ○ The ruler can either try to keep them happy (difficult) or get rid of them (nearly impossible without causing chaos).

Why Persia Was Easy to Control After Alexander Won

King Darius III led the Persian Empire much like the Ottoman Empire. There was one strong ruler and appointed officials to help govern. Once Alexander defeated Darius, there were no independent noble families left to challenge him. Since Persians were accustomed to absolute rule, they simply accepted Alexander as their new king, as long as order was maintained.

Had Alexander's generals stayed united, ruling Persia would have been easy. Instead, they fought among themselves for power.

Why Rome Had a Harder Time Controlling Conquered Lands

Rome had a much harder time ruling places like Spain, France, and Greece. Unlike Persia, these lands had many small kingdoms and noble families. Even after Rome conquered them, the people remained loyal to their old rulers and kept rebelling.

It took many years for Rome to fully control these regions. Only when all former ruling families were gone and the people got used to Roman rule did things finally settle down.

Key Lesson

Alexander's empire stayed together not just because of his skill as a leader, but because of how Persia was structured.

- States ruled by one central leader (like Persia) are hard to conquer but easy to control once taken.
- States ruled by many powerful nobles (like France) are easy to conquer but hard to control afterward.

This is why some leaders, like Pyrrhus of Epirus, struggled to hold onto their lands, while Alexander succeeded. Knowing these differences helps rulers make better choices when they grow their power.

Modern Reflections on Chapter 4: Why Alexander's Successors Kept Control of Persia

1. Some Systems Are Harder to Overthrow Than Others

Machiavelli says some governments are easy to take over but tough to manage. A kingdom ruled by a single leader may be difficult to overthrow, but if that leader is removed, the entire system can collapse. In contrast, a land with many powerful nobles is easier to conquer but harder to govern due to ongoing resistance.

This applies today in business and politics. A company with a strong CEO may struggle after that leader leaves. A company with multiple decision-makers may enjoy more long-term stability. The lesson? Leaders must know the systems they work in before making big changes.

2. Removing the Old Leadership Can Prevent Rebellion

Alexander the Great's successors kept control of Persia by getting rid of the old ruling family. Without a former king or royal family, there was no strong opposition.

This is relevant in business takeovers as well. When a company is acquired, old leadership can resist new directions. Many new CEOs replace top executives to prevent resistance to new strategies. The key lesson? Change is simpler when the old leadership is gone.

3. Uniting People Under a Common System

Machiavelli points out that people in Persia accepted Alexander's rule. They were used to following one strong leader. This made them more willing to follow his successors.

Today, groups with strong leadership usually stay organized and avoid chaos. A company or government with a strong system allows for smoother transitions. The takeaway? Stability comes from structure, not just from individuals.

5

HOW TO RULE CITIES THAT WERE USED TO FREEDOM

A ruler who conquers a city that was once self-governing faces a unique challenge: its people remember their freedom and will resist foreign rule. To keep control, a ruler has three options.

1. Destroy it completely.
2. Move there and rule directly.
3. Let it keep its own laws but install loyal leaders and collect taxes.

The third option can work because a small group of local rulers, knowing they depend on the prince, will stay loyal. A city used to freedom often accepts rule better from its own people rather than outsiders—but this method is risky.

History Shows That Former Republics Are Hard to Control

Two major examples show why allowing a self-governing city to continue under its own laws is dangerous. First, Sparta tried to control Athens and Thebes by installing loyal rulers, but both cities eventually rebelled.

Second, Carthage is one of the clearest examples of why republics must be destroyed if they are to be ruled effectively. After the Second Punic War, Rome defeated Carthage. Carthage had to follow strict rules to continue existing. As Carthage started to improve its economy, Rome worried about a possible rebellion. In the Third Punic War, Rome completely destroyed the city, ensuring it would never rise again as a threat. This decision showed that as long as a republic stays whole, it will always want to reclaim its independence.

Rome thought it could manage Greek cities by letting them keep their local governments. This approach backfired. Greek city-states, such as Corinth and Athens, still resisted Roman rule. Eventually, Rome had to step in forcefully. They either imposed direct rule or, in some cases, destroyed rebellious cities entirely. This failure showed that having partial control over a former republic can lead to ongoing instability.

Why Former Republics Always Resist

The only guaranteed way to control a former republic is to destroy it completely. If a city that once ruled itself is allowed to survive, it will always try to regain its freedom. People will always remember their past freedom, even if treated fairly. Memories of self-rule create resentment. This makes them eager to rebel at the first chance.

Example: Pisa was ruled by Florence for 100 years, but as soon as it had the chance, it rebelled.

On the other hand, cities that have always been ruled by a prince are much easier to govern. When a ruling family dies out, the people are used to having a leader and often struggle to choose a new one, making them more likely to accept a new ruler.

However, not all republics resist with the same intensity. A newly formed republic may not yet have strong traditions of independence and could be easier to control. In contrast, an older republic with a long history of self-rule will never forget its past and will fight fiercely to restore its freedom. The longer a people have governed themselves, the harder it is to keep them under foreign rule.

Because of this, a ruler should either destroy them completely or live there and govern directly—anything in between leads to constant rebellion.

Modern Reflections on Chapter 5: How to Rule Cities That Were Used to Freedom

1. People Never Forget Freedom

Machiavelli says that cities used to ruling themselves are the hardest to control. Even if a ruler treats them well, they will always want their independence back. We see this in history when countries stand up to colonizers. It also happens when workers resist corporate takeovers.

In modern life, this applies to companies that try to take away work-from-home policies. Employees who had freedom before will push back against new restrictions. The lesson? Once people have experienced freedom, taking it away is almost impossible without a fight.

2. The Three Ways to Control an Independent Group

Machiavelli gives three ways to rule a city used to freedom:

1. Destroy it completely.
2. Move there and govern it directly.
3. Let them keep their own government but make them dependent on you.

This applies to leadership today. When a company buys a startup, the new owner has a few choices. They can shut it down, send their own managers to take charge, or keep the original team but control their funding. Every method has its risks and benefits. Machiavelli warns that partial control can often spark rebellion.

3. People Will Always Fight to Restore Their Way of Life

A ruler who takes over a free city might think that after a few years, people will forget their past independence—but they won't. People, like returning employees, cling to traditions and values. They bring back what they loved.

The takeaway? Leaders who ignore history and tradition will struggle to control those who still remember the past.

6

NEW LEADERS WHO GAIN POWER THROUGH SKILL AND STRENGTH

Why Great Leaders Succeed

Some of history's greatest leaders rose to power through skill, not luck. People often try to follow the paths of those before them, just as an archer aims slightly above his target to account for a weak bow. Those who aim too cautiously will always fall short, while those who set ambitious goals—even if they do not fully reach them—will still achieve far more than the timid. It is better to strive boldly and miss the mark slightly than to aim too low and achieve nothing of worth. A prince must act in this way, setting his sights high and never hesitating when fortune presents an opportunity. Even if they don't reach the same heights, aiming high gets them closer.

A leader's success depends on how he gains power. If he rises through ability, the beginning is hard, but staying in power becomes easier. If he rises through luck, success may come easily, but holding onto it is much harder.

Skill vs. Luck in Leadership

Great rulers like Moses, Cyrus of Persia, Romulus, and Theseus didn't rely on luck alone. They seized opportunities, but their skill helped them turn chances into lasting success.

- Moses led the Israelites out of slavery because their suffering made them eager to follow him.
- Romulus grew up outside Alba and used his outsider status to become Rome's legendary founder.
- Cyrus saw that his people were unhappy and used their discontent to take over Persia.
- Theseus brought together scattered communities to unite Athens.

Each of them recognized the right moment to act and had the skill to make it happen.

The Challenge of Creating a New System

A leader who builds a new government or introduces major changes will face strong resistance. People fear change, and those who benefited from the old system will fight to keep it. At the same time, those who might gain from the new system are often too cautious or uncertain to fully support it.

To succeed, a leader must not rely on persuasion alone.

People are easily convinced in the moment, but their loyalty fades over time. If a leader doesn't have the strength to enforce his rule, he will fail.

History proves this point:

- Moses, Cyrus, Theseus, and Romulus had the military power to secure their rule.
- Savonarola, a religious leader in Florence, failed because he relied only on words. Once people lost faith in him, he had no way to maintain control.

His failure was inevitable, for a ruler who depends on words alone is like a soldier who enters battle without a weapon. Savonarola spoke grandly and persuaded the people of Florence to overthrow their rulers, but once the moment of passion passed, he had nothing with which to hold power. He had neither arms nor allies. His enemies, knowing this, struck quickly, and when his words failed him, he had no means of defense. He was executed—proof that those who rule by the people's favor alone will not last unless they can back their position with strength.

No great leader secures power through words alone. It is necessary not only to inspire loyalty but also to remove those who might challenge the new order. Moses, in his wisdom, put to death those who opposed his divine mission. Romulus, to strengthen his claim to rule, killed his own brother Remus. Cyrus and Theseus, too, eliminated their rivals to ensure no force could rise against them. A prince who seeks lasting power must understand this: where force is needed, it must be used swiftly and completely, for those who hesitate in dealing with threats will find their own downfall close behind.

Gaining power is tough. However, a leader who removes rivals and secures control early will find it easier to hold onto that power.

The Example of Hiero of Syracuse

Hiero of Syracuse, an ordinary man who became ruler through ability, is a good example. The people of Syracuse, struggling under outside rule, chose him as their leader, and he proved himself worthy.

To secure his rule, Hiero:

- Built a new, loyal army.
- Formed alliances that suited his needs.
- Took full control of both military and political power.

It was hard to rise to power, but staying in power became easy. He eliminated threats and strengthened his position.

A leader who simply takes power is no more than a conqueror; a leader who establishes a lasting system of rule is a true prince. It is not enough to remove the old order—one must build new institutions to secure the future. Those who benefited from the past regime will resist change with all their might, while the common people, uncertain of what is to come, will hesitate to commit fully to the new ruler. This is why Moses gave laws, why Cyrus reorganized Persia, and why Romulus laid the foundations of Rome itself. They understood that a prince who does not shape the future risks being undone by it.

～

Modern Reflections on Chapter 6: New Leaders Who Gain Power Through Skill and Strength

1. Great Leaders Rise by Seeing Opportunity

Machiavelli discusses leaders like Moses, Cyrus, and Romulus. They succeeded by recognizing the right moment to act. They didn't just rely on luck—they used skill and strategy to create their own success.

This happens today with entrepreneurs. Steve Jobs and Elon Musk didn't wait for the right time. They created their own chances and inspired others to believe in their vision. The lesson? Success doesn't just happen; it's created by those who are prepared.

2. Words Alone Are Not Enough

Machiavelli warns that leaders who rely only on words, like Savonarola in Florence, will fail. He convinced people to follow him, but when things got difficult, he had no real power, and his enemies easily removed him.

We see this in politics when leaders give great speeches but fail to take strong action. A company that promises innovation but fails to deliver will lose customers. The key takeaway? Talk is cheap—real leadership requires action and strength.

3. Change Brings Enemies, and Leaders Must Be Ready

When a leader tries to introduce something new, those who benefited from the old system will resist. Meanwhile, those who might gain from the change are often hesitant.

This occurs in politics when governments seek big reforms. It also happens in business when a company starts a new way of working. People naturally fear change. Machiavelli's advice? A leader must expect resistance and be strong enough to push forward anyway.

7

GAINING POWER WITH THE HELP OF OTHERS

Some people become rulers because of luck rather than effort. While it is easy for them to gain power, it is much harder to keep it. This occurs when a person is given control of a state as a gift or reward. For example, the Persian king Darius appointed Greek rulers to govern cities on his behalf. It also applies to those who gained power by bribing or manipulating soldiers.

These rulers depend on the people who put them in charge, but luck and favors are unreliable. Since they were never leaders before, they lack experience, and they don't have strong armies loyal to them. Like a tree with weak roots, their rule can easily be overturned unless they quickly build a strong foundation.

Two Examples: Francesco Sforza and Cesare Borgia
Francesco Sforza: Gaining Power Through Skill

Francesco Sforza became Duke of Milan through hard work and intelligence. He struggled to gain power, but once he did, he kept it easily because he built a strong and stable rule on his own abilities.

Cesare Borgia: Gaining Power Through Luck

Cesare Borgia, also known as Duke Valentino, became powerful because of his father, Pope Alexander VI. Even though he was clever and made smart decisions, he lost power after his father's death. His story shows that even a strong leader can fail if his power comes from someone else's fortune rather than his own skill.

Cesare Borgia's Struggles

Pope Alexander VI wanted to make his son Cesare powerful, but he faced challenges:

- He couldn't give him land belonging to the Church without making enemies.
- Powerful families like the Orsini and Colonna controlled Italy's armies.
- The Pope allowed the French to enter Italy, using them to help Cesare take Romagna.

Once Cesare had control of Romagna, he had to secure his rule. His two biggest problems were:

1. The Orsini and Colonna families, who might turn against him.
2. The French king, who could take back his support at any time.

How Cesare Borgia Tried to Keep Power

Cesare took bold steps to make himself stronger:

- He brought Orsini and Colonna nobles into his service so they wouldn't betray him.
- He tricked and captured Orsini leaders at Senigallia, removing them as threats.
- He gained the trust of Romagna's people by ruling with firm but fair leadership.

Romagna had been poorly governed for years, full of crime and disorder. Cesare put Remirro de Orca, a strict and ruthless leader, in charge to bring peace. Once order was restored, Cesare had Orca publicly executed to show that he was not cruel like his minister. This won him the support of the people.

Cesare Borgia's Downfall

After securing his power, Cesare's biggest problem was the King of France, who had started to see him as a threat. Cesare wanted to be free from French help. Then, his father, Pope Alexander VI, died unexpectedly.

Cesare had worked to protect himself by:

- Getting rid of rivals who could challenge him.
- Winning the loyalty of Rome's nobility and cardinals.
- Strengthening his army so he could fight off enemies.

However, when his father died, Cesare was sick and unable to act quickly. Even though he had built a strong foundation, luck turned against him, and he lost everything.

Cesare was a smart and fearless leader. Even after losing power, the people of Romagna stayed loyal to him. His enemies couldn't remove him immediately. He even managed to block the election of a pope who would completely oppose him.

If he had been healthy when his father died, he might have been able to hold onto power. He later said that he had planned for everything except his own sudden illness. His downfall was not due to a lack of skill but bad luck.

Cesare Borgia's story teaches us a key lesson: leaders who get power by chance must move fast to keep it. Though he made few mistakes, his reliance on fortune ultimately led to his downfall.

∽

Modern Reflections on Chapter 7: Rising to Power Through Luck and the Help of Others

1. Power Given by Others Is Unstable

Machiavelli warns that leaders who gain power through luck or outside help struggle to keep it. This is like a CEO who is promoted just because of family ties—if they don't prove their skill, they will quickly fail.

The lesson? If you inherit power, you must work hard to show you deserve it. If you rise through luck, you must develop real abilities to keep it.

2. Cesare Borgia: A Near-Perfect Strategy—Ruined by Bad Luck

Cesare Borgia was a skilled leader, but he relied too much on his father, Pope Alexander VI. When his father died, his power collapsed.

This is like a business leader who depends too much on one investor or a politician who relies on a single ally. If that support disappears, they fall. Machiavelli's lesson? Leaders must build their own strength, not depend entirely on others.

3. Always Prepare for Leadership Transitions

One of Cesare Borgia's biggest mistakes was not securing a friendly successor for his father. In business and politics, not planning for leadership changes can ruin all that has been built.

The lesson? A great leader not only builds power but also ensures the future is secure after they are gone.

8

GAINING POWER THROUGH CRUEL MEANS

There are two ways a private citizen can become a ruler without relying entirely on luck or skill. One involves gaining power through harsh and illegal means. The other happens when people select a leader. We'll focus on the first case. We'll look at two historical examples: one from ancient times and another more recent. We won't judge their morality. Those in similar situations may find these examples useful.

Agathocles of Syracuse: Seizing Power Through Mass Murder

Agathocles of Sicily was born into poverty as the son of a potter but rose to become King of Syracuse. Though he led a criminal life from an early age, he was both physically strong and highly intelligent. He chose a military career and climbed the ranks to become a commander. Then, he decided to take power for himself.

The Seizure of Power

He secretly teamed up with Hamilcar, the Carthaginian commander in Sicily. One morning, he called a meeting with the Senate and top citizens of Syracuse. He pretended it was about state affairs. At his signal, his soldiers stormed in and slaughtered them. With no opposition left, he took control of the city.

Maintaining Control

Agathocles faced military defeats and a siege from Carthage. Still, he defended Syracuse well. Then, he even attacked Carthage itself. This forced Carthage to withdraw and recognize his rule over Sicily.

Agathocles didn't rise by luck. His success came from his strong determination and smart, tough strategies. While he was bold and skilled, his cruelty and betrayal prevent him from being called virtuous. His success came from a calculated use of brutality, not luck or traditional virtue.

Oliverotto da Fermo: Betrayal and Murder at a Banquet

A more recent example comes from the era of Pope Alexander VI. Oliverotto da Fermo, an orphan raised by his uncle Giovanni Fogliani, trained as a soldier under Paolo Vitelli. He was ambitious and skilled. But he became unhappy serving others. So, he sought power for himself.

The Betrayal

Oliverotto teamed up with Fermo's powerful citizens who liked tyranny. He plotted his takeover. He wrote to his uncle, claiming he wished to visit his hometown and display his military achievements. Giovanni, proud of his nephew, welcomed him with honor and arranged a grand reception.

Days later, Oliverotto threw a grand banquet. He invited Fermo's top citizens. After dinner, he shifted the talk to politics. He praised Pope Alexander VI and his son, Cesare Borgia. He then suggested continuing the discussion privately. Once in a separate room, his hidden soldiers emerged and slaughtered the guests, including his uncle.

The Downfall

With his rivals eliminated, Oliverotto seized the city. Over the next year, he tightened his grip on power. However, his success was short-lived. Cesare Borgia, famous for getting rid of rivals, tricked Oliverotto into coming to Senigallia. There, Oliverotto was captured and executed. He faced the same betrayal he had used before.

The Proper and Improper Use of Cruelty

Why did Agathocles stay in power while Oliverotto lost it so fast? The answer lies in how they used cruelty.

Well-Used Cruelty

- Applied decisively in a single stroke
- Should not be repeated to avoid prolonged fear and instability
- Necessary violence carried out all at once, followed by fair governance
- Agathocles used this plan—he acted quickly with his first atrocities. Then, he worked on solidifying his power.

Poorly Used Cruelty

- Starts small and continues over time
- Breeds instability and resentment
- Forces a ruler to rely on fear indefinitely
- Oliverotto made this mistake, leading to his downfall

A ruler should apply cruelty swiftly and decisively. The initial shock allows people to regain a sense of security.

Acts of kindness should be introduced gradually to maximize goodwill. The shock fades, and the people can regain a sense of security. Acts of kindness, on the other hand, should be introduced gradually to maximize goodwill.

A ruler using this strategy can keep stability and avoid ongoing repression. Those who fail will always live in fear, forced to wield violence endlessly. Waiting too long to punish enemies will look like weakness, not strength. This makes the action useless.

Modern Reflections on Chapter 8: Rising to Power Through Evil Means

1. Ruthlessness Can Bring Power, but Not Respect

Machiavelli talks about leaders like Agathocles. He used harsh violence to gain power. However, he was never viewed as truly great.

This is like business leaders who fire entire teams to cut costs. They might save money, but they damage their reputation. The takeaway? Cruelty can bring success, but it won't earn trust or lasting respect.

2. If You Must Be Cruel, Do It Quickly

Machiavelli says a ruler who needs to be harsh should do it all at once, so people can recover. But kindness should be given in small amounts over time.

This applies to tough decisions in leadership. If layoffs are needed, they should happen all at once—not dragged out for months. But rewards should be given gradually to keep morale high. The key lesson? When difficult actions are necessary, do them fast—then focus on rebuilding trust.

9

GAINING POWER THROUGH THE SUPPORT OF THE PEOPLE

How a Private Citizen Becomes a Prince

Some rulers rise to power not through violence or luck, but with the support of the people. This is a civil principality. It needs political skill, not just luck or special talent.

A prince can gain power in one of two ways:

• With the help of nobles—who hope he will protect their interests.
• With the support of the common people—who seek protection from oppression.

Ruling with the Nobles vs. Ruling with the People

- A prince supported by nobles struggles more because nobles see themselves as equals and may resist his rule.
- A prince backed by the people rules easily. He holds power alone, with no rivals to challenge him.

The people only want to avoid oppression, while nobles desire power over others—making them harder to satisfy. A prince must recognize that he will always be outnumbered by the people and should work to secure their loyalty.

How a Prince Should Handle Nobles

Nobles fall into two categories:

1. Loyal nobles – These should be honored and trusted.
2. Uncertain nobles – These require closer attention:

    - If hesitant due to fear, they can be reassured.
    - If driven by ambition, they are dangerous and should be treated as enemies.

A prince backed by the nobles must win over the people to strengthen his rule. If he protects them, they may become even more loyal than if they had originally supported him.

The Importance of Popular Support

A prince who has the people on his side is far stronger in times of crisis.

Nabis, Sparta's ruler, faced attacks from Greeks and Romans. He survived thanks to the support of his people. If they had turned against him, no military force could have saved him.

Some say relying on the people is unstable, claiming *"He who builds on the people builds on mud."* However, this is only true for weak leaders. A true prince who knows how to command and prepares for crises will find that popular support is a solid foundation.

The Risk of Governing Through Magistrates

A civil principality can struggle when it tries to become an absolute rule. A prince may govern:

- Directly—holding power himself.
- Through magistrates—officials who enforce laws.

Relying too much on magistrates is risky because:

- They can turn against him in times of crisis.
- People may be loyal to the magistrates, not the prince.
- In hard times, the prince may find himself without true supporters.

A wise prince does not assume loyalty in good times will last in bad times. When everything is stable, people make grand promises. But when trouble comes, many disappear. Since a ruler only gets one chance to test their loyalty, he must prepare in advance.

How to Secure Long-Term Loyalty

A prince must ensure that his people always need him. They will remain loyal if they depend on his leadership for stability, safety, or success, even when times are hard.

Modern Reflections on Chapter 9: Gaining Power Through the Support of the People

1. People's Support Is Stronger Than the Nobility's

Machiavelli explains that rulers can gain power with the help of either the nobles or the common people. Nobles are tricky because they have their own ambitions. The people, however, just want a leader who won't oppress them.

In politics today, leaders who appeal to the general public have a stronger base than those who rely only on wealthy donors. In business, companies that focus on customers instead of just investors often last longer. The lesson? Winning over the people gives a leader more security than relying on elites.

. . .

2. Leaders Must Make Themselves Necessary

A leader should make sure people rely on them. If people feel they need a ruler, they will stay loyal.

This applies in careers too—employees who make themselves essential to a company are harder to replace. The takeaway? Security comes from being needed.

10

MEASURING THE STRENGTH OF A PRINCIPALITY

Can a Prince Defend Himself?

prince must determine whether he can stand alone or if he needs outside help for protection.

• A self-sufficient prince has plenty of soldiers and resources. This allows him to defend against any attack.
• A weaker prince must rely on allies, as he lacks the strength to fight alone.

If a ruler cannot meet his enemy in open battle, his best option is to fortify his cities and secure the loyalty of his people. A strong city defense keeps attackers away. Long sieges can be expensive and uncertain.

The Strength of German Cities

German cities are a great example of strong, independent states. Though they control little land beyond their walls, they remain safe because they are:

- Well-fortified with strong walls, moats, and artillery.
- Stocked with supplies to last a full year.
- Economically stable, ensuring people have work and do not turn against their leaders.
- Concentrated on military defense. It involves strict rules and training.

These preparations make them hard to attack. Enemies must retreat in failure.

How to Maintain Morale During a Siege

Some worry that citizens will lose faith in their ruler if their lands outside the city are destroyed. But a strong leader can keep morale high by:

- Giving them hope that the siege will not last long.
- Reminding them of the enemy's cruelty, making surrender seem worse.
- Cracking down on those spreading fear or doubts.

When the enemy burns the countryside, the people must

defend their city. Surrender won't bring back what they lost. People tend to be more loyal when they make sacrifices. A prince who prepares well will find it easier to keep that support.

Modern Reflections on Chapter 10: Measuring the Strength of a Principality

1. A Leader Must Be Strong Enough to Stand Alone

Machiavelli says some rulers can defend themselves. Others always need outside help. The strongest leaders are those who can survive without relying on others.

This is true in business, too. A company with strong finances can handle crises better than one that always needs investors to survive. The lesson? Independence creates stability.

2. A Strong Defense Can Prevent Attacks

Machiavelli praises strong cities. He believes they are too expensive for enemies to attack.

Today, this is true for cybersecurity. Companies with strong security systems are less likely to get hacked. It also applies to jobs. A person who keeps improving their skills is less likely to get replaced. The takeaway? Preparation and strong defenses make you a harder target.

11

ECCLESIASTICAL STATES

Why Religious States Are Unique

Ecclesiastical states are not like any other principalities. Once acquired, they are the easiest to maintain.

Unlike other rulers, popes do not need armies to defend their lands or strong policies to keep their people in line. These states rely on religion and traditions. This gives them security, regardless of how they are governed.

Because their power is seen as divine, popes remain in control regardless of circumstances. It's helpful to look at how the Church gained political power. Before Pope Alexander VI, it had little influence in Italy.

How the Church Gained Political Power

Before France's invasion of Italy under Charles VIII, the region was controlled by five main powers:

1. The Pope
2. Venice
3. The Kingdom of Naples
4. The Duke of Milan
5. Florence

Their two main goals were:

- Keeping foreign powers out of Italy
- Preventing any one state from gaining too much control

To contain Venice, Italian rulers formed alliances. They supported Rome's noble families, the Orsini and Colonna. This kept the Pope weak. The two families were always in conflict, which stopped the Pope from gaining power.

For years, popes struggled to free themselves from these powerful families. Papal reigns were short, often about ten years. So, no pope had enough time to fully eliminate these factions. This kept the Church politically weak for centuries.

The Turning Point: Pope Alexander VI

Pope Alexander VI changed everything. He was the first pope to show what money and military force could achieve.

Alexander used his son, Cesare Borgia, and the French invasion to weaken the Roman nobility. This also helped him expand the areas controlled by the Church. While he aimed to strengthen Cesare's power, his actions ultimately made the papacy far stronger than before.

Pope Julius II: Expanding the Church's Strength

Julius II inherited a much stronger Church and built on Alexander's success. His major achievements included:

- Conquering Bologna
- Defeating Venice
- Expelling the French from Italy

Unlike Alexander, who worked for his son's benefit, Julius focused on strengthening the Church itself. He also kept the Orsini and Colonna families weak, preventing them from regaining power.

Pope Leo X and the Future of the Church

Leo X inherited a papacy that was now the most powerful institution in Italy. His challenge was not just to survive. It was to boost its prestige with wisdom and strong leadership.

Modern Reflections on Chapter 11: Ecclesiastical Principalities

1. Power Backed by Tradition and Belief Is the Strongest

Machiavelli points out that religious leaders, such as the Pope, gain power from faith and tradition. People obey them not due to strong armies but because they believe in their authority.

This still rings true today. Brands like Disney or Harvard maintain power because people trust their legacy. They don't need to fight for recognition; it's already theirs. The lesson? Belief in the institution behind you strengthens your power.

2. When People Believe in a System, They Defend It Themselves

Religious leaders often do not encounter rebellion like other leaders do. Their followers support their authority.

We see this in political movements and loyal brands like Apple. Apple users promote and defend the brand willingly. The key takeaway? When people believe in a leader or system, they become its strongest defenders.

12

THE DIFFERENT TYPES OF MILITARY FORCES

A ruler must have a strong foundation to keep power, and that foundation depends on good laws and a strong military. Without a good army, laws mean little. This chapter focuses on military forces and the types of soldiers a prince can use.

A ruler can have various types of soldiers: his own army, hired mercenaries, borrowed troops from allies (auxiliaries), or a mix of these. Mercenary and auxiliary troops can be risky and untrustworthy. A ruler who depends on mercenaries will never have real security. These soldiers lack organization, show untrustworthiness, and often act cowardly in battle. They act brave when there is no danger but run away when facing real threats. They are loyal only to their paycheck, not to the prince. A ruler who relies on them will be robbed in times of peace and defeated in times of war.

The Problems with Mercenaries

Italy's weakness came from relying too much on mercenaries. For years, Italian rulers hired soldiers instead of training their own armies. These mercenaries were good at fighting each other, but when real enemies invaded, they failed. This is why King Charles of France was able to conquer Italy so easily.

There are two types of mercenary leaders:

- Skilled leaders: If they are talented, they will try to take power for themselves.
- Unskilled leaders: If they are weak, they will cause the prince to lose battles.

Either way, mercenaries are dangerous. The safest army is one that belongs to the ruler himself. If a republic hires a general, it must have strict rules to keep him from becoming too powerful.

Examples of Mercenary Failures

Strong states have always used their own armies. In contrast, those that relied on mercenaries often faced problems. For example:

- Carthage hired mercenaries but nearly lost everything in the fight against Rome.

- Thebes: Hired Philip of Macedon, who later took over their land.
- Milan: Hired Francesco Sforza to fight for them, but he later turned against them and took power.
- Naples: Queen Giovanna hired mercenaries. They abandoned her, so she had to rely on the King of Aragon. He then took control.

Even when mercenaries brought victories, it was often because of luck. Florence avoided disaster. Its hired generals were not ambitious, faced tough opponents, or had different goals.

Why Italian Mercenaries Were Weak

Italy grew weak when cities and republics stopped training their armies. They began hiring mercenaries instead. At first, this seemed like a good idea, but over time, the problems became clear:

- Mercenary armies were too small and ineffective in real wars.
- Their commanders avoided danger, caring more about money than victory.
- Battles became slow and indecisive, with little risk for either side.

As a result, stronger foreign armies often invaded and

embarrassed Italy. Mercenary soldiers focused on comfort rather than victory. This choice caused Italy's downfall.

Now that we understand how mercenaries weakened Italy, we need to look at how they became so popular in the first place. By studying their rise and growth, we can learn from past mistakes and find better ways to protect a country.

Modern Reflections on Chapter 12: The Different Types of Military Forces

1. A Leader Must Rely on Their Own Strength, Not Others'

Machiavelli warns that rulers who rely on mercenaries or borrowed troops will fail. Soldiers fighting for money lack loyalty.

This applies to business too. Companies relying on outside contractors become weak. The lesson? Build strength from within. A leader needs a dedicated team invested in success.

2. Loyalty Matters More Than Talent

Machiavelli says that mercenaries leave their leaders when the going gets tough. The same is true in modern leadership. Hiring skilled workers won't help if they don't care about the company's mission.

The best leaders foster loyalty. Employees who believe in

their company work harder than those just after a paycheck. The takeaway? A dedicated team is more valuable than a talented but unreliable one.

13

AUXILIARY TROOPS (BORROWING ANOTHER LEADER'S ARMY)

Why Auxiliary Troops Are Even Worse Than Mercenaries

Auxiliary troops are soldiers lent by another ruler. For instance, Pope Julius II used Spanish troops to fight Ferrara. Auxiliaries can be well-trained, but they pose a serious risk to any ruler who depends on them.

- If they lose, the prince is defeated.
- If they win, the prince is now at their mercy.

History offers many examples of auxiliary troops leading to disaster:

- Pope Julius II came close to losing everything when Spanish forces faltered at Ravenna. He was saved just in time by Swiss reinforcements.

- The Florentines sent 10,000 French troops to capture Pisa but ended up in greater danger than before.
- The Byzantine Emperor brought Turkish soldiers into Greece for a local war. When the fighting stopped, they wouldn't leave and took control of the area.

A prince who relies on auxiliary forces risks failure. They may be disciplined, but they follow a different master. It's better to fight and lose with your own army than to win with foreign troops. Relying on them can lead to dependence.

Cesare Borgia: A Lesson in Military Independence

Cesare Borgia's rise and fall illustrate the dangers of relying on outside forces:

1. He started with French troops, using them to capture cities like Imola and Forlì.
2. He hired mercenaries from the Orsini and Vitelli families. However, they proved to be unreliable.
3. He built his own army, eliminating his mercenaries and creating a force loyal only to him.

At each stage, his power grew stronger. With French troops, he was weak. With mercenaries, he was vulnerable. But with his own forces, he was truly feared.

A similar story comes from Hiero of Syracuse, who saw

his mercenaries were untrustworthy. Instead of keeping them, he had them executed and relied only on citizen soldiers. The Bible shows this lesson too. When David got ready to fight Goliath, King Saul gave him a sword and armor. But David turned them down and chose to use his simple weapons instead.

The Mistake of Relying on Foreign Troops: France's Example

King Charles VII of France created a permanent national army after driving out the English. However, his son, Louis XI, abandoned this system and relied on Swiss mercenaries instead. This made France:

- Weaker, as its own army declined.
- Dependent on the Swiss, to the point where France could neither fight without them nor fight against them.

Had France continued Charles VII's military reforms, it would have been invincible. Short-term ease caused long-term risk—like a slow disease that's ignored until it's deadly.

The Fall of Rome: A Warning Against Outsourcing Defense

The Roman Empire began its decline when it stopped using its own soldiers and relied on foreign mercenaries. Over time, Rome's power faded, and the barbarian tribes—once hired as auxiliaries—overran the empire.

This proves a timeless truth:

"Nothing is as weak or unstable as the reputation of power that relies on forces not its own."

Lessons for Rulers

A state is only truly secure when it has its own military. Leaders who depend on borrowed power are gambling with their survival. To build lasting strength, follow leaders like Philip of Macedon. He trusted his own people instead of foreign forces.

Modern Reflections on Chapter 13: Auxiliary Troops (Borrowing Another Leader's Army)

1. Borrowing Power Creates More Problems Than It Solves

Machiavelli warns that relying on another country's army is even worse than hiring mercenaries. If they win, you owe them. If they lose, you remain defenseless.

This applies to business and politics today. A company relying too much on another's technology is vulnerable. A politician tied to a strong ally may lose power if that ally disappears. The lesson? Relying on others for strength is risky.

. . .

2. If You Do Not Control Your Own Power, Someone Else Will

Machiavelli says that if you let others fight for you, they gain control.

This happens in leadership too. A business relying on investors instead of building profits allows investors to call the shots. A politician who lets donors shape policies isn't truly independent. The key takeaway? A leader who doesn't control their own power isn't a true leader.

14

WHAT A LEADER MUST FOCUS ON

The Importance of Military Skill

A prince should be obsessed with the art of war—it is the foundation of power. Military strength not only helps rulers keep their states but also allows ambitious men to rise from nothing.

History shows that rulers who ignore military matters often lose their power. Francesco Sforza earned the title Duke of Milan with his military skill. But his sons chose luxury over discipline, and they lost everything.

Disarmament leads to disrespect and insecurity. An unarmed ruler can't control an armed population. His subjects will see him as weak, and he will always live in fear. Without military strength, he cannot earn the loyalty of his soldiers or the respect of other rulers.

How a Prince Should Train for War

Even in peacetime, a prince must prepare for war in two ways: physical action and study.

1. Physical Training

- A ruler should keep his troops well-trained and maintain personal endurance.
- Hunting helps a prince build strength and understand the land. He learns about mountains, rivers, and plains, which are important for strategy.
- Knowing the terrain helps him defend his land. It also lets him navigate foreign areas well.

Philopoemen was a Greek general. He always studied military strategy. When traveling, he would ask his companions:

- *"If our army were here and the enemy was on that hill, who would have the advantage?"*
- *"How should we attack or retreat?"*

By thinking this way even in peacetime, he was always prepared for war.

2. Studying Military History

○ A prince should learn from great military leaders—how they fought, won, and failed.
○ He should copy successful leaders but steer clear of the mistakes made by those who failed.

Examples:

- Alexander the Great modeled himself after Achilles.
- Julius Caesar admired Alexander.
- Scipio Africanus studied Cyrus the Great and used his strategies to defeat Carthage.

Rulers use this method to turn knowledge into power. This way, they stay ready and never get caught off guard.

Why Constant Preparation is Essential

A prince who wastes peacetime in idleness will fail when war comes. Those who prepare in advance can endure hardships, while those who do not will collapse under pressure.

Modern Reflections on Chapter 14: What a Leader Must Focus On

1. Leaders Must Always Be Prepared for Hard Times

Machiavelli says a good leader should think about war, even in peace. Waiting for a crisis means it's too late.

In today's world, this applies to businesses, governments, and careers. Companies that prepare for downturns last longer than those that spend recklessly. Workers who keep learning won't panic if they lose jobs. The lesson? Always prepare for challenges before they arrive.

2. A Leader Should Always Stay Sharp

Machiavelli says rulers must study history and train constantly. A lazy leader gets caught off guard.

This applies to modern CEOs, politicians, and athletes. The best leaders improve continuously. The key takeaway? Great leaders never stop learning and preparing for the future.

15

WHETHER IT'S BETTER TO BE LOVED OR FEARED

The Reality of Leadership

Now that we have discussed how a prince should rule, we must consider how he should conduct himself. Some philosophers talk about ideal rulers with perfect virtue, but such rulers have never existed.

A prince who acts according to how people should behave, rather than how they actually behave, will be ruined. The world is full of deception, ambition, and selfishness. A ruler must know when to act morally and when to abandon morality for the sake of survival.

Reputation vs. Reality

People judge rulers based on qualities such as:

- Generosity or greed
- Mercy or cruelty
- Honesty or deceit
- Weakness or strength
- Kindness or arrogance
- Religious devotion or indifference

Ideally, a prince would possess all the good qualities and avoid all the bad ones. But this is impossible. Instead, he must be practical:

- Avoid vices that would destroy his power.
- Embrace some vices if they help him maintain control.

What seems virtuous can lead to downfall, while what seems immoral can ensure stability. A wise ruler does not ask, *"Is this good or bad?"* but rather, *"Will this keep me in power?"*

Modern Reflections on Chapter 15: Whether It's Better to Be Loved or Feared

1. Good Leaders Must Be Respected, Not Just Liked

Machiavelli argues it's better to be feared than loved. A leader who is only loved may be ignored in tough times.

In modern workplaces, a boss trying too hard to befriend

employees may struggle with tough decisions. A respected leader, even if not loved, maintains order. The lesson? It's nice to be liked, but being taken seriously is more important.

2. Fear Can Work, but It Must Be Controlled

Machiavelli warns that a leader should not be hated—just feared enough to maintain respect. Too much cruelty leads to revolt.

This applies in business too. A strict but fair manager fosters productivity. A harsh boss drives employees away. The key takeaway? Being firm is good—being cruel is dangerous.

3. People Are Selfish—Leaders Must Accept This

Machiavelli believes most people act in their own interest. A leader expecting loyalty and gratitude may be disappointed.

This holds true in politics and business. Employees leave for better jobs. Customers switch brands for better deals. The best leaders don't expect endless loyalty; they create an environment where people want to stay. The lesson? Instead of complaining about selfishness, smart leaders plan for it.

16

GENEROSITY AND MISERLINESS

The Danger of Excessive Generosity

It is good for a prince to be seen as generous, but trying too hard to maintain this reputation will lead to ruin.

To appear generous, a ruler must spend lavishly, quickly exhausting his resources. When his money runs out, he will be forced to raise taxes, making him unpopular and hated. When a crisis hits, he will struggle to respond. His treasury and the goodwill of his people will be depleted.

If he tries to cut back on spending, he will still be criticized—now as a miser.

Why a Wise Prince Embraces Frugality

A ruler should not fear being called miserly. In fact, this reputation is far more useful than being known as generous.

- A frugal prince can govern without burdening his people with heavy taxes.
- He will have resources to defend his state and fund military campaigns when necessary.
- Over time, people will see that his careful spending ensures stability and prosperity.

History shows that rulers who manage resources wisely succeed. In contrast, those who are too generous often lose their power.

Pope Julius II gained power through generosity. However, once he became pope, he cut back on spending and shifted his focus to war. The Kings of France and Spain funded long wars without overtaxing their people. They did this by being careful, not wasteful, with their money.

When Generosity Works and When It Fails

- Generosity is useful for gaining power—Julius Caesar used it to build support during his rise.
- But once in power, generosity can be risky if not managed well.

A prince can be generous when using others' wealth. For instance, a military leader rewards his soldiers with war spoils. Alexander the Great, Julius Caesar, and Cyrus the Great all did this successfully.

When a ruler uses his own resources, his generosity can

backfire. The more he gives, the less he has. This often leads him to raise taxes or cut benefits, which causes resentment.

A prince should avoid being hated. Too much generosity can cause hatred. It makes a ruler take from his people to keep up appearances.

The Smarter Approach: A Reputation for Frugality

It is better for a ruler to be known as careful with money (miserly) rather than wasteful (generous).

- Misers may be criticized, but they are not hated.
- Generous rulers may end up taking from their people. This can cause resentment.

True generosity isn't just giving handouts. It's about using resources wisely. This approach helps create stability, security, and long-term prosperity.

Modern Reflections on Chapter 16: Generosity and Miserliness

1. A Leader Who Spends Too Much Will Eventually Run Out

Machiavelli warns that rulers who give too much will soon run out of resources. They may then need to raise taxes or take harsh actions to maintain power, leading to public backlash.

This is seen today in politics and business. When governments overspend, they can end up in debt. This often leads to economic crises. CEOs who provide excessive perks without planning risk having to cut jobs later. The lesson? Smart leaders handle resources wisely. They focus on long-term success while protecting their people.

2. It's Better to Be Seen as Cautious Than to Go Broke

People might grumble if a leader is tight with money. They will complain more if careless spending leads to financial trouble.

This applies to personal life as well. Someone who treats friends to lavish meals might seem generous initially, but debt will catch up with them. The key takeaway? Real generosity comes from stability, not from quick spending.

17

CRUELTY VS. MERCY

The Role of Cruelty in Leadership

E very prince would prefer to be seen as kind rather than cruel. However, excessive kindness can lead to disorder. Cesare Borgia was feared, yet his harshness brought peace and stability to Romagna. In contrast, the Florentines, avoiding cruelty, allowed Pistoia to fall into chaos.

This proves that a little cruelty can be more merciful than unchecked leniency. A ruler who refuses to make tough decisions may allow greater suffering in the long run.

As Virgil wrote in *The Aeneid*: "Harsh necessity and the challenge of ruling a new kingdom force me to act this way and secure my borders with strict discipline."

However, cruelty must be used wisely. A prince should

not act on every rumor or suspicion, nor be reckless. He must strike a balance between decisiveness and restraint.

Should a Ruler Be Loved or Feared?

Ideally, a prince should be both loved and feared. But since this is rare, if forced to choose, it is far safer to be feared than loved.

- Love is unreliable. People are ungrateful and self-serving. They will support a ruler when it benefits them but abandon him in times of crisis.
- Fear is more dependable. People will obey a leader they fear, even when it is in their best interest to betray him.

However, a prince must avoid being hated. A ruler can be feared without being despised if he does not:

1. Seize people's property
2. Harm their families

History shows that men will forgive the death of a father more easily than the loss of their wealth. If punishment is necessary, it should be justified and understood as necessary for the greater good.

When is Cruelty Necessary?

Discipline is crucial in military leadership. Without it, no army remains strong.

- Hannibal controlled a large and varied army in foreign lands. He earned this through respect and fear. His strict leadership prevented internal rebellion.
- Scipio, in contrast, was too lenient, allowing his troops too much freedom, leading to mutiny in Spain. The Roman Senate even criticized him for hurting military discipline.

Harsh but fair leadership brings order. In contrast, too much kindness can create chaos.

Final Answer: Choose Fear, But Avoid Hatred

Since love is unreliable but fear is consistent, a wise ruler should build authority on fear rather than love. He should not be hated. If he respects his subjects' property and families, he can be feared without being despised.

This balance is the key to lasting power.

Modern Reflections on Chapter 17: Cruelty vs. Mercy

1. A Leader Should Be Firm, but Not Hated

Machiavelli says being feared can help a leader, but they should avoid being hated. If people hate their leader, they will seek to remove them.

This holds true in workplaces, too. A strict but fair boss commands respect, while an overly harsh one breeds resentment and low morale. The lesson? Leaders need to enforce rules but also show understanding.

2. Mercy Can Sometimes Cause More Harm Than Strictness

Machiavelli warns that being too soft can lead to exploitation. He points out that disorder can grow in cities. Too much mercy may lead to more violence because people don't fear the consequences.

In today's world, this applies to law enforcement, business, and parenting. A company that misses deadlines will have a hard time being productive. A society that avoids tough decisions may face larger issues later. The takeaway? Leaders must strike a balance between kindness and control to prevent chaos.

18

WHETHER RULERS SHOULD KEEP THEIR PROMISES

Is Honesty Always the Best Policy?

Many believe that a ruler who keeps his promises and leads with honesty deserves praise. History shows that rulers who use deception and manipulation often do better than those who lead with strict integrity. Leaders who break promises when needed often outsmart those who never do.

The Two Ways to Fight

There are two ways to fight and survive in power:

1. Through laws – The way of humans, relying on rules and agreements.

2. Through force – The way of animals, using strength and power.

Laws alone are not always enough to protect a ruler. He must also know how to use force when necessary. Ancient writers showed this idea through Chiron the centaur. He raised famous rulers, including Achilles. The centaur—half man, half beast—represents the need for a prince to be both intelligent (human) and strong (animal).

A prince must balance the qualities of:

- The lion – Powerful, but easily trapped.
- The fox – Clever enough to avoid traps but too weak to fight off enemies.

A wise ruler must be both. He must be strong enough to command respect (like a lion) but also smart enough to recognize danger before it happens (like a fox).

When a Prince Should Break His Word

A prince who relies only on brute force will fail. A ruler must be prepared to break his promises when keeping them would put him at a disadvantage. It might sound wrong, but people can be dishonest. So, a ruler may have good reason to use deception against them.

Rulers have often made treaties and agreements. Then, they break them when it benefits their interests. Those who were best at deception often ended up winning. However, a prince must never break his word openly—he must disguise his dishonesty well.

Example: *Pope Alexander VI* never kept his promises, yet people always trusted him. He mastered the art of deception, and it worked in his favor every time.

The Importance of Appearing Virtuous

A prince doesn't need to actually have all the good qualities people admire—he just needs to appear to have them. It is useful for a ruler to be seen as:

- Merciful
- Faithful
- Honest
- Kind
- Religious

However, he must be ready to act against these virtues whenever necessary. If he blindly follows moral ideals at all times, he will be destroyed. A prince should always do good when possible, but be willing to do evil when necessary.

Controlling Public Perception

A prince should never openly show his ruthless side. Instead, he must always act and speak as if he embodies mercy, faith, and honesty.

Of all the virtues, appearing religious is the most important.

People judge based on what they see, not what is actually true:

- Everyone sees how a ruler appears; few know the truth.
- Those few who do know the truth will stay silent because the majority believes what they see.

In politics, results matter more than promises. If a prince is successful and keeps power, people will see his actions as justified.

We see this today in certain leaders (whom I won't name). They talk about peace and honesty, yet they are the most cunning and deceitful of all. If they truly followed their moral principles, they would have lost power and respect.

Modern Reflections on Chapter 18: Whether Rulers Should Keep Their Promises

1. A Leader Should Be Honest—But Not Naïve

Machiavelli says a leader should seem honest. However, they shouldn't always keep promises if it puts them at a disadvantage.

This is relevant in business negotiations. A company may promise a deal, but if the other side breaks their word, should they still comply? A leader who clings to promises risks being taken advantage of. The lesson? A good leader is trustworthy yet adaptable.

2. Image Matters as Much as Actions

Machiavelli argues that a leader's appearance matters more than always being good. This reflects a truth in leadership—people judge based on perception.

This is why politicians craft their public images, and companies focus on branding. Innovative businesses draw in investors, even if not much changes behind the scenes. The takeaway? Leaders must manage both reality and perception to maintain their power.

19

AVOIDING HATRED AND CONTEMPT

The Key to Stability: Avoiding Hatred and Contempt

A prince must avoid two great dangers: hatred and contempt. If he can escape these, his rule will remain stable, even if he has other flaws.

• Hatred comes from greed—seizing wealth or dishonoring women. A ruler must never do this.
• Contempt comes from weakness—being seen as indecisive or cowardly. A ruler must always project strength and decisiveness.

A respected ruler does not tolerate internal plots or outside dangers.

Managing Internal and External Threats

A prince faces two main dangers: rebellion from within and attacks from outside.

- A strong military and alliances guard against foreign threats.
- Public support defends against conspiracies. People won't back plotters if they respect their leader.

History shows that conspiracies often fail. They rely on secrecy, but conspirators usually betray one another. This happens as they try to win the ruler's favor. If a prince is beloved, the public will punish conspirators themselves.

Balancing Nobles and Common People

A ruler must manage the ambitions of the nobles while keeping the people satisfied. Wise rulers create institutions to balance power, as seen in France's parliament, which:

- Prevents nobles from becoming too powerful.
- Reassures the common people that they are protected.

A prince should give unpopular tasks to others. He should keep the popular actions for himself. This helps him maintain goodwill.

Lessons from the Roman Emperors

Roman emperors had to tackle special challenges. They balanced power between the nobility, the people, and the military. Those who failed to manage these groups often lost their rule.

- Weak but well-meaning rulers, such as Pertinax and Alexander Severus, were ousted by their own troops.
- Cruel rulers like Commodus and Caracalla caused fear and hate. This led to their assassinations.
- Septimius Severus succeeded by blending strength with cleverness. He won the army's loyalty and kept order among the people.

Modern rulers must balance power. They need to prioritize the group with the most influence. At the same time, they must keep goodwill with others.

Final Thoughts

A ruler's downfall often comes from mismanaging power—either being too weak or too brutal. A new prince must:
1 Use strength and deception to establish control.
2 Transition to fairness and justice once power is secure.

This balance stops both too kind and too cruel rulers from failing. It helps ensure a strong and lasting reign.

Modern Reflections on Chapter 19: Avoiding Hatred and Contempt

1. A Leader's Worst Enemy Is Public Hatred

Machiavelli warns leaders can survive being feared, but if they are hated, they are at risk. People will seek any chance to overthrow them.

This occurs today in business and politics. A CEO making unpopular decisions may face backlash. A politician who loses public trust may struggle to remain in office. The key lesson? A leader can make tough choices but must avoid becoming the enemy of those they lead.

2. People Will Forgive Many Things—But Not Disrespect

Machiavelli says rulers often get overthrown if they humiliate or insult others. Even poor policies can be tolerated, but public disrespect lingers.

This applies in leadership today. A strict but respectful manager retains loyal employees. However, one who mocks their team will quickly lose support. The takeaway? A leader must be strong while treating others with dignity.

20

WHETHER FORTRESSES HELP OR HURT A LEADER

Different Strategies for Securing Power

Princes have used different ways to keep control, such as:

- Arming or disarming their subjects.
- Encouraging division among the people.
- Turning enemies into allies.
- Building or demolishing fortresses.

There is no single right answer—each strategy depends on the specific circumstances of the state.

Arming vs. Disarming the People

A new prince should never disarm his subjects. History shows that rulers who arm their people gain:

- Loyalty—subjects who bear arms feel personally invested in their leader's success.
- Security—armed citizens are less likely to rebel.

If a prince gains new land, he should disarm the locals. He can keep weapons with those who helped him. Allies should also be weakened over time. This helps stop them from becoming a threat.

Disarming subjects creates distrust and hatred. The prince becomes weak and depends on mercenaries. But mercenaries are not a reliable solution, as we discussed before.

Dividing the People: A Risky Strategy

Some rulers foster internal divisions. They think a divided population is easier to control. However, this is a short-term tactic that often backfires.

Venice kept its subject cities split between Guelf and Ghibelline factions. This stopped them from uniting against Venetian rule. When Venice lost at Vailà, one faction quickly revolted.

A divided state is weak in times of crisis because:

- One faction will side with an enemy.
- The other faction will not be strong enough to resist alone.

Encouraging division works in peacetime but fails in war—a prince should avoid relying on it.

Using Enemies to Strengthen Power

Struggles and opposition often help a prince prove his strength. Fortune can make enemies for new rulers. They can then strengthen their power by defeating these foes.

Example: Pandolfo Petrucci of Siena relied more on former enemies than on old allies. Why? Those who opposed him worked hard to show their loyalty. Meanwhile, his longtime supporters grew complacent.

A prince should carefully analyze his situation:

- Enemies who once depended on him may become his strongest allies.
- Enemies who only joined him out of hatred for the previous ruler will never be truly loyal.

Are Fortresses Useful?

Rulers often build fortresses. They do this to guard against rebellion or invasion. While they provide security in some cases, they can also create a false sense of safety.

Some rulers have even torn down fortresses to strengthen their control:

• Niccolò Vitelli destroyed fortresses in Città di Castello to prevent enemies from using them.
• Duke Guidobaldo of Urbino did the same after reclaiming his territory from Cesare Borgia.
• The Bentivogli family removed fortresses in Bologna to limit threats.

When Fortresses Help vs. When They Hurt

• If a prince fears foreign enemies more than his people, fortresses may be useful.
• If a prince fears his own people more than external threats, fortresses will not protect him.

Example: Francesco Sforza built a fortress in Milan, but it alienated the people and later became a tool for his enemies.

The best fortress is not being hated by the people. If the people oppose a prince, they will find foreign allies to help remove him. This makes fortresses pointless.

One rare case where a fortress worked: Caterina Sforza survived an assassination attempt in Forlì by holding out in a fortress. When Cesare Borgia attacked, the fortress failed. The people sided with him. Her real weakness was losing their support.

Final Thoughts on Fortresses

Building or destroying fortresses depends on circumstances. But no prince should rely on them alone. A leader who trusts in walls while allowing himself to be hated is making a fatal mistake.

Modern Reflections on Chapter 20: Whether Fortresses Help or Hurt a Leader

1. A Leader Who Trusts Only Walls Will Be Trapped

Machiavelli says some rulers build fortresses for safety. But if the people hate them, those walls won't help.

This applies to business and politics today. A leader who isolates from criticism will face bigger problems. A CEO who hides behind bureaucracy may lose control. The key lesson? Real security comes from support, not isolation.

2. Winning the Support of the People Is the Best Defense

Machiavelli argues that the strongest leaders earn loyalty, not rely on walls or armies. If people support you, walls become unnecessary.

This idea works in all areas. Business leaders, community figures, and friends thrive when people trust them. The takeaway? Focus on building strong relationships instead of just defense.

21

HOW A LEADER GAINS HONOR

Gaining Respect Through Great Actions

A prince earns the most respect by taking on big projects and proving his strength through bold decisions. A great example is Ferdinand of Aragon, King of Spain. He started as a weak ruler, but through ambition and smart strategies, he became one of the most powerful kings in Europe.

Looking at his reign, we see a series of daring moves. His first major achievement was conquering Granada. This victory expanded his kingdom and kept the powerful Castilian nobles too busy to plot against him. At the same time, he gained control over them without them realizing it.

Ferdinand also increased his power by:

- Using money from the Church and the public to build a strong army.
- Starting wars in the name of religion, such as forcing converted Jews (Marranos) out of Spain.
- Leading military campaigns in Africa, Italy, and France—all under the excuse of defending the faith.

By constantly taking bold actions, Ferdinand kept his people in awe. They were too distracted to rebel against him, and his victories created a cycle of success that made him unstoppable.

Using Rewards and Punishments to Build Authority

A prince should also leave a strong impression by making big public decisions. For example, Messer Bernabò of Milan became famous for his firm and unforgettable leadership. A prince should react when someone does something very good or very bad. People need to notice this response. He can give generous rewards or impose harsh punishments. This builds his reputation and reminds people of his power.

Every decision a prince makes should show that he is a skilled and capable leader.

The Risk of Staying Neutral

A prince earns respect not just by being bold but also by choosing a side in conflicts. He should always make it clear whether he is a friend or an enemy—never remain neutral.

When two nearby states go to war, a prince may hesitate, worrying about who will win. But staying neutral is usually a mistake:

- The winner will see the prince as weak and may attack him next.
- The loser will be angry that he didn't help and won't trust him in the future.
- He will end up alone, with no allies to protect him later.

History provides a clear example. When King Antiochus invaded Greece, he asked the Achaeans, allies of Rome, to stay neutral. Rome, however, demanded they take up arms. A Roman envoy warned:

"If you stay out of this war, you will be left without friends and without honor. In the end, you will just be a prize for the winner."

This lesson fits all conflicts. Enemies want neutrality, but allies want action. A prince who refuses to take a side may avoid short-term problems but will usually suffer in the long run.

Why Choosing a Side is the Smarter Move

If a prince supports an ally and they win:

- Even if they are stronger, they will owe him for his help.

- They won't want to betray someone who stood by them.
- Even the most powerful victors have limits—they need allies and must keep their promises.

If the prince's ally loses, they will still try to help him in return. History shows that even defeated nations can rise again.

If both sides in a war are weak, supporting one is even more useful. By helping one, the prince weakens the other and gains an ally who depends on him.

Avoid Becoming a More Powerful Leader's Pawn

A key rule is to never team up with a much stronger ruler unless you have to. If a prince does, even victory will leave him at the mercy of his ally.

For example, Venice joined France in attacking Milan when they could have stayed neutral. This decision led to their downfall. Sometimes, alliances are necessary. For example, Florence had to align with Spain and the Pope against Lombardy. In such cases, a prince must carefully consider the risks.

No political choice is ever without risk. Leadership is about recognizing which option is the least dangerous and making the right call.

Gaining Public Support and Encouraging Prosperity

A prince also wins respect by supporting hard work, talent, and economic growth. He should:

- Encourage skilled workers and reward those who excel.
- Promote trade, farming, and other productive activities.
- Protect people's property so they don't fear unfair taxes or government seizures.

Instead of taxing too heavily and harming the economy, a prince should reward those who contribute to the state's wealth.

A prince should also hold festivals, celebrations, and public events at the right times. Cities are often organized into guilds or social groups, so he should engage with these groups. He must be approachable but still maintain the dignity of his position.

Modern Reflections on Chapter 21: How a Leader Gains Honor

1. Bold and Decisive Leaders Earn Respect
Machiavelli advises rulers to act boldly to gain honor.

Staying safe may prevent trouble, but it won't lead to greatness.

This applies to business and politics today. Leaders who take risks—like trying new ideas or entering new markets—often enjoy lasting success. The lesson is clear: being too cautious can be just as risky as being bold.

2. Supporting Others Can Strengthen Your Own Power

Machiavelli thinks leaders should choose sides in conflicts, not remain neutral. Supporting the right people builds strong alliances.

This is true in modern leadership. A CEO who helps key employees grow builds loyalty. A politician who stands by allies during tough times gains support later. The takeaway? Supporting others makes a leader stronger.

22

THE IMPORTANCE OF GOOD ADVISORS

Why Choosing the Right Advisors Matters

A prince's success depends a lot on the people he surrounds himself with. One of the first ways people judge a ruler's intelligence is by looking at his advisors. If they are wise and loyal, the prince is seen as smart for picking them. If the advisors are weak or selfish, the prince will look foolish. Choosing poor advisors is a big mistake for any leader.

A great example is Antonio da Venafro, who advised Pandolfo Petrucci, the ruler of Siena. People thought Pandolfo was a wise leader. They believed this because he chose Antonio, who was highly skilled.

Three Types of Thinkers

There are three levels of intelligence:

1. Those who think for themselves – The smartest minds.
2. Those who recognize good ideas in others – Still very capable.
3. Those who neither think for themselves nor recognize good ideas – Useless.

A prince may not need the highest intelligence. He should at least have the second highest. This means he must recognize good advice and strong advisors. If he can judge their work fairly, rewarding good service and correcting mistakes, his ministers won't be able to mislead him.

How to Spot a Bad Advisor

There's an easy way to tell if an advisor is bad:

- If he cares more about himself than the prince, he is untrustworthy.
- If he always seeks personal gain, he will never serve the state well.

A good advisor must focus on the prince's success and the state's well-being. They should not let personal ambition distract them.

How a Prince Should Treat His Advisors

To keep his advisors loyal, a prince must:

- Respect them – Show appreciation for their service.
- Reward them – Pay them well so they don't seek wealth elsewhere.
- Make them dependent on him – Give them responsibilities and privileges they wouldn't have without him.

When an advisor knows that his success depends on the prince, he will remain loyal. He won't want a new ruler, because his wealth, power, and safety are all tied to the current leadership. If this balance is broken, both the prince and his advisors will struggle.

Modern Reflections on Chapter 22: The Importance of Good Advisors

1. A Leader Is Only as Strong as Their Inner Circle

Machiavelli warns that poor advisors can ruin a ruler. Leaders must choose wise, loyal counselors and avoid flatterers.

This is relevant today. CEOs with strong teams make better choices. Presidents who have strong advisors handle crises better. The lesson? Smart, honest people lead to success.

2. A Wise Leader Asks for Advice—but Decides for Themselves

Machiavelli says rulers should listen to advice but must make final decisions. Relying too much on others can make them seem weak.

This applies now. A business leader who lets consultants make all the decisions loses control. The takeaway? Good leaders listen but don't let others rule them.

23

AVOIDING FLATTERERS

The Danger of Flattery

One of the biggest risks for a ruler is being deceived by flattery. In royal courts, many people will say whatever the prince wants to hear to gain favor. Since most people enjoy being praised, even a smart ruler can fall for false compliments.

However, avoiding flattery is tricky. If a prince allows everyone to speak freely, he might lose their respect. But if he discourages honesty, he will never hear the truth.

How a Wise Prince Handles Flattery

A smart prince should take a balanced approach:

- Choose a small group of trusted, intelligent advisors.
- Give them permission to speak the truth—but only on topics the prince asks about.
- Regularly consult them on all major decisions.
- Make it clear that honest opinions are welcome and won't be punished.

Outside this group, the prince should avoid listening to too many opinions. Once he has made a decision with his advisors, he should act confidently and not keep changing his mind.

The Problem with Indecisiveness

A ruler who listens to too many different voices will appear weak because he constantly changes his mind. A good example of this mistake is Emperor Maximilian. His ambassador, Pre' Luca, once said:

"The emperor never asks for advice, yet never follows his own plans."

Maximilian kept his ideas secret, but whenever he started acting on them, his advisors disagreed. He lacked the confidence to follow through, making him seem uncertain and unreliable. People didn't trust his leadership because he was always changing direction.

Good Leaders Make Their Own Decisions

Some believe that a prince is only considered wise because of his advisors. This is not true. In reality:

- A wise prince will attract good advisors.
- A foolish prince cannot be saved, even by the best advisors.

If a weak ruler gathers many advisors, they will compete for power and put their own interests first. Since the prince cannot judge their advice properly, they will manipulate him. Even if he has only one strong advisor, that person may eventually take control and replace him.

Because people naturally act in their own self-interest, a prince must have the intelligence to lead on his own. Good advice is only useful if the ruler himself is capable of making wise decisions.

Modern Reflections on Chapter 23: Avoiding Flatterers

1. Leaders Must Beware of Empty Praise

Machiavelli cautions that some advisors use flattery to gain favors from rulers. Leaders need to identify honest feedback versus empty praise.

This occurs in business when employees praise a bad

boss just to keep their jobs. In politics, advisors might avoid tough truths. The key lesson? Leaders should welcome honest feedback, not just praise.

24

WHY LEADERS LOSE POWER

A New Ruler Must Secure His Power

If a new prince follows the advice I've given, he will establish his rule as firmly as if he had been in power for years. In fact, he may be even stronger than someone who inherited their position. A new ruler faces more scrutiny, but if he proves himself capable, people will respect him more than a ruler who simply comes from a long line of kings.

People care more about their present situation than the past. If they are doing well under the new ruler, they will be content and won't demand more. As long as the prince governs wisely, the people will defend him. This earns him double honor:

1. For successfully taking power.

2. For strengthening his rule through good laws, a strong military, and smart leadership.

On the other hand, a prince who is born into power but loses it due to poor leadership earns double disgrace.

The Mistakes of Italy's Fallen Princes

Many Italian rulers lost their states because they made the same mistakes. Some examples include the King of Naples and the Duke of Milan. Their two biggest failures were:

- Weak military strategy – They failed to build and maintain strong armies.
- Poor political control – They either angered the people or couldn't manage the nobility. Even if they had public support, they lacked the power to keep control.

A ruler with a strong army and a stable government is very difficult to overthrow.

A good example of strong leadership is Philip of Macedon (not Alexander the Great's father, but the one defeated by the Romans). Despite facing powerful enemies, Philip managed to keep his kingdom for years. He was able to do this because he:

- Led wisely and made smart decisions.

- Kept the people on his side by maintaining their loyalty.
- Controlled the nobles and prevented them from gaining too much power.

Even when he lost battles, he still managed to hold onto his kingdom.

Failure to Prepare Leads to Disaster

The Italian princes who lost their states didn't fall because of bad luck. Their failure was their own fault. During peaceful times, they didn't prepare for future dangers. This is a common mistake—people don't think about storms when the sky is clear.

So when trouble came, instead of defending themselves, they ran away. They hoped that once the people grew tired of their new rulers, they would invite them back.

This was a weak strategy because:

- No ruler should expect others to restore them to power—it almost never happens.
- Even if they do return, they won't have control over their own fate.
- A ruler who depends on outside help is always vulnerable.

Only leaders who rely on their own strength and strategy can build a lasting and stable rule.

Modern Reflections on Chapter 24: Why Leaders Lose Power

1. Ignoring Problems Will Lead to Collapse

Machiavelli explains that rulers often lose power by ignoring warning signs and failing to act.

We see this in companies that won't change and in politicians who overlook public discontent. The takeaway? Problems don't disappear—strong leaders address them early.

25

THE ROLE OF LUCK IN LEADERSHIP

Does Fortune Control Everything?

Many people believe that luck or fate decides everything, leaving no room for personal effort. History is full of surprises, so this belief has become more popular. Some conclude that since they can't control events, they should simply accept whatever happens.

Even I have considered this idea. However, I believe that while fortune plays a role, it does not control everything. If luck determines half of our lives, the other half—or at least a large part—remains in our hands.

Fortune is Like a Raging River

Fortune can be compared to a powerful, flooding river. When it overflows, it destroys everything in its path—trees, buildings, and farms—forcing people to run for safety. In moments like this, it seems unstoppable.

However, when the river is calm, people can prepare. They can build dams and barriers to control its force and reduce damage when the next flood comes.

The same applies to fortune. She is strongest where people fail to prepare. A well-organized state—like Germany, France, or Spain—can resist the forces of luck. But Italy, which did not build its defenses, was easily swept away by changing events.

Why Some Leaders Suddenly Lose Power

It's common to see a leader who seems secure one day but is overthrown the next, even though they didn't change their behavior. This usually happens for two reasons:

> 1. Relying too much on good luck – A ruler who depends only on fortune will collapse when luck turns against him.
> 2. Failing to adapt – A leader who thrives now may struggle when times change. If they resist adjusting, they will face challenges.

People achieve success in different ways:

- Some are cautious, others are bold.
- Some use force, others use strategy.
- Some are patient, others act quickly.

All of these methods can work, but only if they match the situation. The problem is that most people stick to what has worked for them in the past, even when times change.

Success Requires Adaptability

A leader who thrives in one era may struggle in another simply because they refuse to change. A cautious ruler will succeed when caution is needed, but if the times call for boldness and he does not adapt, he will fail.

People rarely change their nature. If they have succeeded by following a certain method, they will continue using it—even when it no longer works. This is why fortune seems so unpredictable.

A truly wise leader would be flexible, adjusting to the demands of the moment. However, such perfect adaptability is rare, which is why even capable rulers sometimes fail.

Pope Julius II: A Bold Leader

Pope Julius II was aggressive in everything he did, and luckily for him, the times suited his boldness. Because of this, he always succeeded.

For example, when he launched his campaign against Bologna while Giovanni Bentivogli was still in power:

- Spain and Venice were unsure about supporting him.
- France had not fully committed.
- The situation was uncertain.

Instead of waiting, Julius acted quickly. His sudden attack caught everyone off guard. The Venetians and Spain hesitated, and the King of France, needing the Pope's support against Venice, felt forced to help him.

If Julius had waited for everything to be perfectly arranged, he would have failed. His ability to seize the moment allowed him to accomplish what a more cautious leader could not. However, his success was partly due to timing. If patience was needed instead of aggression, his approach wouldn't have worked. Fortunately for him, he died before facing such a challenge.

Fortune Favors the Bold

Success depends on a leader's natural tendencies matching the changing times. Those who succeed are simply those whose personal style fits the moment.

That said, if one must choose between boldness and caution, boldness is better.

Fortune is like a woman—she must be handled with strength and determination. She favors those who take action rather than those who hesitate.

- Bold leaders take risks and shape events.

- Cautious leaders wait and are controlled by events.

Fortune favors young men for their energy and boldness. It also rewards rulers who are aggressive and willing to take charge.

Modern Reflections on Chapter 25: The Role of Luck in Leadership

1. Fortune Favors the Bold

Machiavelli compares luck to a river—when calm, leaders must prepare for floods. Those who wait for luck will be swept away in a crisis.

This holds true today. A business that prepares for downturns will survive tough times. An athlete training year-round will be ready for big games. The lesson? Luck matters, but preparation is key to success.

2. The Best Leaders Adapt to Change

Machiavelli argues leaders must adjust based on the times. A cautious leader may succeed in one era but fail in another that needs boldness.

Today, this applies to companies that resist change. Blockbuster failed while Netflix adapted. The takeaway? Those who refuse to change will be replaced by those who do.

26

A CALL FOR A STRONG LEADER

Italy's Need for a Strong Leader

After everything I've discussed, I've asked myself: Is now the right time for a great leader to rise and restore Italy's honor? My answer is yes—there has never been a better moment.

History shows that great leaders emerge during times of crisis:

- Moses grew into a great leader after the Israelites endured slavery in Egypt.
- Cyrus could not have proved his strength if the Persians had not been oppressed by the Medes.
- Theseus became a hero because the Athenians were weak and divided.

Likewise, Italy's suffering has created the perfect moment for a leader to unite the nation. Italy is more enslaved than the Hebrews, more oppressed than the Persians, and more divided than the Athenians. It has no strong leadership, no unity, and is constantly looted and humiliated by foreign powers.

Italy is Ready for Change

Many before have tried to free Italy, only to be stopped by bad luck. Now, the nation is barely holding on, waiting for a leader who can heal its wounds and put an end to:

- The destruction of Lombardy.
- The taxation and oppression of Naples and Tuscany.
- The cruelty and arrogance of foreign rulers.

The Italian people are desperate for freedom. They are ready to follow anyone who will raise a banner for their independence.

The Right Leader for the Job

Now is a crucial time. No family is better for this task than yours. Your house is strong due to fortune, merit, and Church support. You have both the opportunity and the responsibility to lead Italy's liberation.

If you follow the example of history's great liberators,

success will not be difficult. They were great men, but they had fewer advantages than you do now. They faced obstacles just as great as yours, and God did not favor them more than He favors you today.

As the Roman historian Livy once said:

"A just war is one that is necessary, and arms are sacred when there is no other hope but in arms."

A New Military for a Stronger Italy

One of the biggest reasons Italy has failed in the past is its lack of a strong, independent army. In history, a strong military and fair laws have given rulers great honor.

Italy has talented soldiers. Individually, they are:

- Strong,
- Agile,
- Skilled.

Yet, in large armies, they fail because their leaders are weak, divided, and lack authority. This has been shown in every major battle with Italian forces in the last twenty years. This includes Taro, Capua, Genoa, Bologna, and Mestre.

Building a Superior Italian Army

If you want to be Italy's great liberator, you must create your own army. No military force is more trustworthy or effective than one made up of its own people, led by its own leader.

The Spanish and Swiss armies are respected, but each has a weakness:

- The Spanish struggle against cavalry.
- The Swiss can be defeated by an army as determined as they are.

A strong Italian army could beat them. It's trained to counter these weaknesses. The Battle of Ravenna showed this clearly. Spanish infantry matched German battalions by using speed and shields. They effectively countered the long pikes of their enemies.

A leader who brings new military strategies will gain power and fame. This will secure Italy's freedom for many generations.

The Time is Now

This moment must not be wasted. Italy has waited too long for a leader to rise. If you step forward, you will be met with:

- Love from the people,
- A thirst for vengeance against foreign rulers,
- Unshakable loyalty from Italians desperate for freedom,
- Tears of gratitude from those who have suffered under foreign rule.

Every city will welcome you. Every Italian will follow

you. No foreign enemy can stand against a united Italy. The foreign rulers stink in everyone's nostrils—their time is over.

A Call to Action

Take up this mission with the courage and hope that great causes demand. Lead Italy to its rightful place of honor so that, under your leadership, the words of the poet Petrarch may finally come true:

"*Against barbarian rage, Virtue will take the field; then short the fight; True to their lineage, Italian hearts will prove their Roman might.*"

Modern Reflections on Chapter 26: A Call for a Strong Leader

1. A Nation in Crisis Needs a Bold Leader

Machiavelli ends *The Prince* with a call for Italy to unite under a strong ruler. He believes only a decisive, skilled leader can save a nation from chaos.

This applies today when countries or companies face crises. People seek leaders who can act, make tough choices, and inspire confidence. The key lesson? Strong leadership is crucial in difficult times.

FINAL TAKEAWAYS FROM THE PRINCE

1. Leadership Is About Control, Not Morality

Machiavelli doesn't focus on what is "right" or "wrong"—he focuses on what *works*. While kindness and honesty are valuable, leaders must first secure their power. A weak leader who tries to be "good" at all times will often be overthrown by someone more ruthless. The real lesson? Leadership is about understanding human nature and using that knowledge wisely.

2. Perception Is as Important as Reality

Machiavelli repeatedly emphasizes that appearing strong is just as important as being strong. In modern times, public figures, CEOs, and politicians carefully manage their image because perception drives trust, loyalty, and power. The best leaders shape how people see them while also maintaining real strength behind the scenes.

3. Fortune Favors the Prepared

Luck plays a role in leadership, but those who prepare for opportunity are the ones who succeed. Whether in politics, business, or personal life, those who anticipate change and adapt quickly will always have the advantage. Waiting for luck to guide you is a mistake—you have to be ready to act when the moment arrives.

4. Power Is Easier to Keep If You Win People's Support

Machiavelli's most practical advice is that a leader should avoid being hated at all costs. Fear can work, but a leader who inspires loyalty will always have a stronger foundation. The takeaway? The best leaders balance strength with trust—they command respect while making people feel protected and valued.

5. Change Is Inevitable—Adapt or Be Replaced

The most important modern lesson from *The Prince* is that leaders who don't evolve will be overtaken by those who do. History is filled with rulers, companies, and industries that failed because they refused to change. Whether leading a nation, a business, or a personal career, the key to lasting success is flexibility, strategy, and preparation for the future.

—

This concludes the modern version of *The Prince*, Machiavelli's timeless guide to power, leadership, and strategy. His insights have shaped rulers, politicians, and leaders for centuries—and now, they're accessible to you.

But the journey of learning doesn't stop here. This book is part of the *For Everyone* series, a collection of history's most important works rewritten in clear, modern language. We bring timeless ideas to life, so you can learn from the world's greatest thinkers without struggling through dense, archaic texts.

The *For Everyone* series explores philosophy, leadership, and personal success—ideas that have influenced generations of rulers, strategists, and decision-makers.

If you found this book helpful, be sure to explore the rest of the series. Each book makes profound insights easy to understand and apply.

Thank you for reading, and remember—power, like success, is not just about luck. It's about understanding human nature, making smart decisions, and applying the right strategies. The wisdom of the past remains just as valuable today, and your journey to mastering it continues.

EPILOGUE

This concludes the modern version of *The Prince*, Machiavelli's timeless guide to power, leadership, and strategy. His insights have shaped rulers, politicians, and leaders for centuries—and now, they're accessible to you.

But the journey of learning doesn't stop here. This book is part of the *For Everyone* series, a collection of history's most important works rewritten in clear, modern language. We bring timeless ideas to life, so you can learn from the world's greatest thinkers without struggling through dense, archaic texts.

The *For Everyone* series explores philosophy, leadership, and personal success—ideas that have influenced generations of rulers, strategists, and decision-makers.

If you found this book helpful, be sure to explore the rest

of the series. Each book makes profound insights easy to understand and apply.

Thank you for reading, and remember—power, like success, is not just about luck. It's about understanding human nature, making smart decisions, and applying the right strategies. The wisdom of the past remains just as valuable today, and your journey to mastering it continues.